Pray Your

Way

To

Divine

Establishment

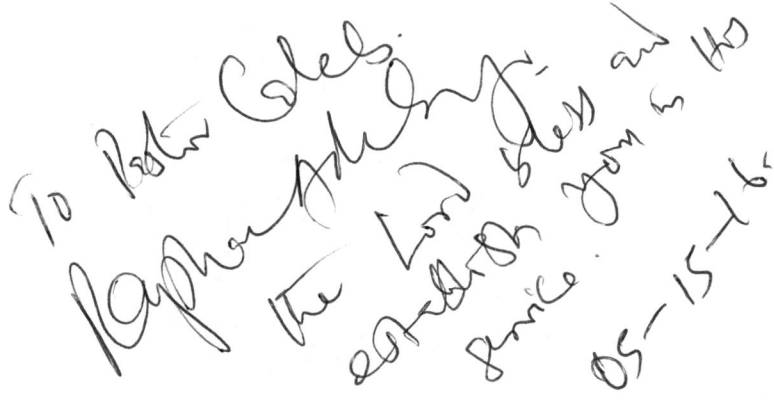

To Pastor Coles;
Raphon Johnson.
The Lord bless and
establish your in His
service.
05-15-16

𝒫ray Your Way To Divine Establishment.

ISBN   978-0-9794876-5-1

Published by WinnersWord Publications.

In the US, write to:
Pastor Raphael Adebayo
RCCG, The Winners Assembly
P O Box 151372
Dallas TX 75215-1372
Telephone: 214-687-2429
www.prayyourway.org

Edited and Desktop Published by
Immaculata Simisola Ngwube
Cover Design by Gbenga Olowo

$\mathcal{D}$edication

To the glory of God of Abraham, Isaac and Jacob, whose free gift of salvation redeemed my soul from eternal destruction, and to those who are thirsty for the move and favor of God.

Acknowledgement

My profound gratitude goes to my mother, Mrs. Bolatito Adebayo, the vessel that God used to bring me to this world, who nurtured me, and whose acceptance of my change in faith from Islam to Christianity, doused the persecution from my siblings and others. My dear wife, Elizabeth Bimpe Adebayo and our lovely children. You accepted me and loved me unconditionally. I will forever love you. I appreciate the contribution of great friends, mentors and fellow laborers in the vineyard of our Lord Jesus Christ towards making this vision possible. Special thanks goes to Dr. R Gary Heikkila. After I shared my testimony with you in Orlando Florida, you sowed a seed of faith that led to the writing of this book.. My special thanks goes to the members of The Redeemed Christian Church of God, The Winners Assembly, your commitment to our ministry is my testimony of divine establishment. You will never lose your reward.

Thank you.

Contents

*I*ntroduction

*T*he word *establishment* is from the root word "*establish*" which means to be settled, to fix firmly, make stable or permanent, to be recognized and accepted, to be rooted and grounded. Divine establishment is an establishment that is ordained by God, the God of Abraham, Isaac and Jacob, the father of our Lord Jesus Christ. One very important characteristic of Divine Establishment is that, it is as a result of deep thoughts and planning of God for His creation, it is never arbitrary or without deliberate effort. Fishes are created to live in water; birds are made to fly in the atmosphere while man is created to live in the Garden of Eden. Fruitfulness and a life of dominion over all other creatures is an unquestionable destiny of man.

God said concerning all His children in book of *Jeremiah:*

Jeremiah29:11 " For I know the thoughts that I think towards you, says the LORD, thoughts of peace and not of evil, to give you a future and a hope." Apostle Paul said in Phil.1: 6 "being confident of this very thing, that He who has begun a good work in you will complete it until the day of Jesus Christ."

Man is designed for success, an image of God in glory and power. God is committed to seeing dreams become reality. *"Faithful is He that calls you who also will do it". 1 Thessalonians 5:24" "Blessed be the God and Father of our Lord Jesus Christ, who has blessed us with every spiritual blessing in the heavenly places in Christ, just as He chose us in Him before the foundation of the world, that we should be holy and without blame before Him in love, having predestined us to adoption as sons by Jesus Christ to Himself, according to the good pleasure of His will, to the praise of the glory of His grace, by which He made us accepted in the Beloved, having made known to us the mystery of His will, according to His good pleasure which He purposed in Himself." Ephesians 1:3-6,9.*

The thoughts of God concerning every individual are communicated through dreams, visions, trance or a small still voice. According to Amos 3:7 *"Surely the Lord GOD does nothing, unless He reveals His secret to His servants the prophets."*

Pharaoh had a dream, which he told Joseph. During the process of interpreting the dream Joseph said, *"the thing is established by God, and God will shortly bring it to pass"* Gen. 41:32. God communicates the things He has established for man through dreams and visions. There is a seed of greatness in every man that propels great dreams. It is often said that a man cannot be greater than his dream. The book of Romans says it more clearly:

Romans. 8:28-30: "And we know that all things work together for good to those who love God, to those who are the called according to His purpose. For whom He foreknew, He also predestined to be conformed to the image of His Son, that He might be the firstborn among many brethren. Moreover whom He predestined, these He also called; whom He called, these He also justified; and whom He justified, these He also glorified."

The life of Joseph can be divided into four stages. 1. Joseph, under the protection and care of his parents and family members. 2. Joseph, as a slave; 3. Joseph, as a prisoner; and, 4. Joseph, as a Prime Minister. Jesus went through these four stages: 1. Jesus, under the tutelage of his earthly parents; 2. Jesus, in the wilderness where he was tempted to sin against God; also a servant to his disciples and humanity; 3, Jesus, as a prisoner in the hand of Pontius Pilate; and finally 4, Jesus, as the Kings of kings and the Lord of lords at the right hand of God the father.

Before any one can achieve the complete will of God they must pass through these stages. It is important to note that Joseph, like Jesus, exhibits the dominion anointing as promised in Gen.1: 28. In any situation Joseph found himself, he did not lack the favor of God.

8

At home with his brethren he was the star, as a slave he had so much favor that his master's wife was begging for his love, in the prison he was the head of the prisoners and lacked nothing. He enjoyed the presence of God and finally in Egypt, he was totally in charge.

The will of God for humanity is to live a life of dominion, but Satan, according to John 10:10, has come to steal, kill and destroy every great plans that God has for man. The intention of Lucifer or the devil is to destroy the abundant joy that God promised man from the beginning of creation. His plan is to turn dreams into nightmares, visions into illusions, prophecies into lies, Garden of Eden to dens of lions. Joseph's dreams was attacked at three levels; Root enemy, Household enemy and Market place enemy; but the favor of God, the giver of dreams, visions and desires of the heart of man, established his dreams.

Despite great attacks against the dreams of Joseph, God was with him all the way. His dreams became realities. He was neither like Moses who saw the land, but could not get there nor like David who wanted to build a house for God but was unable to. He was like Jesus Christ who accomplished the total counsel of God for His life. Pains and death could not prevent Him. This book will use the life of Joseph, the eleventh son of Israel to address spiritual roadblocks to the attainment of joy that surpasses all understanding. Prayer points are raised after each section to invoke divine establishment in every area of your life. It is my prayer that you will not die with your best music in you. You will sing all of it in the land of the living in Jesus name, Amen!

Chapter One

Joseph's Dreams of Greatness

*J*oseph was Rachel's son for Jacob, and the eleventh of twelve sons. Jacob preferred Rachael to Leah his first wife, whom he reluctantly accepted as wife. Stories of Jacob's (also known as Israel) marital life can be found in Genesis 29- 31. Joseph was the beloved of his father.

Gen.37: 3-11: <u>*3 Now Israel loved Joseph more than all his children, because he was the son of his old age. Also, he made him a tunic of many colors.*</u> *4 But when his brothers saw that their father loved him more than all his brothers, they hated him and could not speak peaceably to him. 5 Now Joseph had a dream, and he told it to his brothers; and they hated him even more. 6 So he said to them,* <u>*"Please hear this dream which I have dreamed: 7 There we were, binding sheaves in the field. Then behold, my sheaf arose and also stood upright; and indeed your sheaves stood all around and bowed down to my sheaf."*</u> *8 And his brothers said to him, "Shall you indeed reign over us? Or shall you indeed have dominion over us?" So they hated him even more for his dreams and for his words. 9 Then he*

dreamed still another dream and told it to his brothers,
and said, "Look, I have dreamed another dream. And
this time, the sun, the moon, and the eleven stars bowed
down to me." 10 So he told it to his father and his
brothers; and his father rebuked him and said to him,
"What is this dream that you have dreamed? Shall your
mother and I and your brothers indeed come to bow
down to the earth before you?" 11 And his brothers
envied him, but his father kept the matter in mind.

Joseph had two dreams, which revealed the mind of God
concerning him. He did not do anything to deserve it nor
did he beg for it. Our God is Almighty! He does as He
pleases. Just as a man will have three dogs or pets and
assign to them different roles as he pleases, God the
great Porter created man with a definite plan for each of
them. The plan of God for Joseph was to be king. He
was to rule and be worshiped, have dominion, be fruitful
and multiply. The earthly things will worship him
(sheaf) so also the heavenly things will also obey him
(sun, moon and the stars). Whatever he binds on earth
shall be bound in heaven, and whatsoever he loosed on
earth shall be loosed in heaven. God wanted to prove the
validity of Genesis 1:28 where God commanded man to
be fruitful and live a life of dominion. God showed him
dreams that communicated His (God's) thoughts towards
him (man). If you can dream it, you can have it. The
mind of God concerning you will not be changed,
vandalized or destroyed in the name of Jesus. The vision

12

is for an appointed time, it will soon speak. Hab. 2: 3. *"Surely the Lord will do nothing, but he revealed his secret unto his servants and prophets"*. Amos 3:7. Dreams are very important in spiritual things. God is a spirit; since man is made in the image of God, God uses dreams as one of the major tools of communication to man.

God communicated his mind to Abram in Gen. 15:1-16, concerning the future of his children, God used dreams to communicate His mind to Mary and Joseph, the earthly parents of our Lord and Savior Jesus Christ. God spoke to Apostle Peter in dreams; the whole book of revelation was a vision that was revealed to John, the beloved. Jesus Christ is the same yesterday, today and forever. *Hebrews 13:8*. Your dreams and visions in any way the Lord brings it to you must be taken seriously. Anytime God speaks in a dream, it appears so real that the dreamer would not forget it. It is always so impressive that the dreamer would not be able to contain it, but desire to share it. Habakkuk admonishes us to write it down and make it plain. Habakkuk 2:2. Keep it in mind; your dream carries important information regarding the plans of God for you. It is my prayer that God will grant you the wisdom needed on how and where to share your dreams.

Joseph shared his dreams with his family and was hated for it. His brothers hated him to death, they hated his guts; how dare God make you a leader over us? He was envied to the point of death. So many times, dreamers always believe that people will buy into their dreams, but most often, that is not the case.

After you share your visions, prepare for battle. Satan will use every power or trick available to him to oppose the vision of God for your life. Satan is never happy to see the glory of God show forth. Satan possessed Cain and he killed his brother; he possessed David and he sent Uraiah to the battlefront to be killed, and possessed Peter to resist the plan of God for Jesus Christ. Anytime you are having the feeling of envy, jealousy or hatred against another person; say to yourself, get thee behind me Satan! The purpose of God for the life of Joseph suffered three deadly blows that will be discussed in the next chapter. It is my belief that the God of Joseph will arise on your behalf to see you to the total fulfillment of your dreams; Amen.

The Root Enemy, Household Enemy, and the Market place Enemy were the three categories of enemies that attacked the plan of God for the life of Joseph. Attack at the foundation through his father (root), through his family members -the brothers (household), and finally at his place of work (market place). Majority of the people confronted with these demonic confrontations do not totally fulfill their destinies. But because Joseph, Jesus Christ, and Apostle Paul fulfilled their Destinies, you will fulfill the total counsel of God for your life in the name of Jesus. Amen.

Chapter Two

Root Enemy

This is the enemy at the very beginning of a life. It could be from one's biological parents or anyone that have direct impact in the life of a child from birth and while growing up. It could also be family traditions or customs that children are made to imbibe or a vow made by parents on behalf of the child or dedication to family altars or affiliations to societies or organizations that do not believe in the name of Jesus as the Savior. According to Psalm 11:3 *"if the foundations are destroyed, what can the righteous do?"* It can only take the favor of God to deliver people from the problem caused to them through their parents, heritage or root. Jacob, through the love he had for Joseph over-exposed him to danger or the wiles of the enemy.

Gen 37: 3-4 "Now Israel loved Joseph more than all his children, because he was the son of his old age. Also he made him a tunic of many colors. *4 But when his brothers saw that their father loved him more than all his brothers, they hated him and could not speak peaceably to him"*. Why did Israel, also called Jacob, have to go to the extent of making Joseph an enviable coat of many colors? Could he not keep this love for his young son in his heart? This singular action of Jacob created more problems for Joseph. Anytime his brothers saw him, they were angry. "Why Joseph, the eleventh child?" must have been the question in their envious minds. If anyone is to be the leader, it should have been Ruben, the first-born son of Jacob. Many of us are suffering from root problems, we inherited problems we knew nothing about, our parents' bragging about us to the wrong ears have caused some deadly attacks we faced and still face in our lives. Some of us that were given "a coat of many colors" in the name of appreciation or commendation from our parents have today become objects of attacks by others.

Many people put words like this on their bumper stickers "Parent of Honor Roll Student", "Employee of the Month," "Crown Prince", to mention a few. All these accolades, as good as they sound, do provoke tremendous spiritual attacks. Satan hates expressions of love and joy. He hates to see man radiating in the fullness of the joy of the Lord. Satan wants people to compromise the ideals of the word of God so they can serve him.

The *coat of many colors* is a worldly identity. We saw David refusing to put on the amour that Saul gave to him to confront Goliath; Daniel also refused to eat the king's meat. Peter gave up multitudes of fish to follow Jesus. Identifying with the world invariably attracts attacks from Satan and his demons. It always separates man from God. Joseph did not know any better because of his age otherwise he would have refused the identity his worldly father Jacob, gave him. Many times, due to lack of spiritual growth one accepts gifts, titles or offers with the thoughts that it may help towards the fulfillment of a vision. No one can help you fulfill your dream, but the one that gave the dream. Those who draw inspirations and revelations through satanic sources to propel dreams and visions must not blame the God of Abraham for a horrible ending. God is able to provide for every vision that He gives. Abram said:

" *I will take nothing, from a thread to a sandal strap, and that I will not take anything that is yours, lest you should say, 'I have made Abram rich".* *God will not share His glory with any man. Gen.14:23*

The first opportunity the brothers had to see Joseph alone, they conspired to kill him. He was always with his father until the occasion demanded for him to be alone. No one is omnipresent but God, the God of Abraham, Isaac and Jacob. The promise of security from any man, organization or nation will fail. Only the Lord of Hosts can ensure an everlasting establishment. The first favor of God towards Joseph in Dothan where they conspired to kill him, was the presence of God. The presence of God caused a division among his brothers. Ruben could no longer agree to their plan to kill him, Judah finds an excuse for him not to be suffocated in a dry well but to be sold. Joseph was then sold to the Midianites who later sold him to Portiphar, an officer in Pharaoh's army.

According to Romans 8: 28 *"And we know that all things work together for good to those who love God, to those who are the called according to His purpose."* The destiny of Joseph according to Gen 15:13 were in Egypt. They unknowingly sent Joseph on his journey to greatness like Jesus Christ was sent on the journey to the right side of the father through the cross. 1 Cor.2: 8 "If they had known they would not have crucified the Lord of glory". Behind every evil-inspired suffering is hidden the glorious agenda of God. The imprisonment of Paul and Silas proclaimed the superiority in the power of the cross, which gave an opportunity to minister the love of God.

Isaiah 43:1-2 *"Fear not, for I have redeemed you; I have called you by your name; You are Mine. 2 When you pass through the waters, I will be with you; And through the rivers, they shall not overflow you. When you walk through the fire, you shall not be burned, Nor shall the flame scorch you."* If your natural or spiritual parent or anyone has "sold you" out like Joseph, in a like manner, the same God that provided Ruben and Judah for Joseph will do the same for you. Your life shall be preserved in Jesus name, Amen.

The coat of many colors for many people is a family altar, traditions, customs, or heritage. Some have been dedicated to other gods contrary to the First Commandment. Some have put a coat of many colors upon themselves through horoscope, familiar spirits, adventures into spirit world and self-effort to gain fame at all cost. Joseph could not embark on his journey to greatness until the coat of many colors was stripped off.

Pray aggressively and say aloud as follows.

1. Father, exonerate me from every root problem that has turned my friends (and relatives) to my enemies in the name of Jesus.
2. Lord Jesus, cut off all roots conducting hatred into my life.
3. I reject every worldly provision that has made people to hate me in the name of Jesus.
4. I will never embark on any errand that will lead to death in the name of Jesus
5. I decree in the name of Jesus that all information about my life in the database of my enemies be deleted.
6. Dogs do not die because they bark; I shall not be killed because of my God-given attributes in the name of Jesus.
7. O Lord, flush out of my system everything that attracts hatred from man and angels in the name of Jesus.
8. I refuse to die before my time in the name of Jesus.

9. O God of Joseph, turn every evil intended for me, to my favor in the name of Jesus.

10. O God, pour the fragrance of your favor into my life so that my life will emit favor anywhere I find myself in the name of Jesus.

Chapter Three

Household Wickedness

Joseph was faced with some of the most violent enemies within the household. Jesus said in Matthew 10:36 *"And a man's foes shall be they of his own household."* An African proverb says it succinctly that *"the insect that is destroying the locust bean tree is at its roots."* Household enemies are very vicious, only the divine favor of God can make a way of escape. It is very similar to the root enemy because they are from people you cannot run away from. A blood tie is not easy to cut off. The only difference between the two is that root enemies may not have evil intentions. Parents that dedicate their sons to idols never meant it for evil. You can only give what you have. Eve did not mean evil when she gave Adam the forbidden fruit in Gen.3:6. Many people suffering from root problems today are usually innocent. For example, I was born into a Moslem family. Albeit I had no choice, yet I suffered untold hardships because of a root that was cursed. If my parents had known they would not have dedicated me to the Moslem faith. Hos. 4:6 says, *"My people perish for lack of knowledge."*

Only life can give birth to life. I decree deliverance from every root enemy confronting you as you read this book in the name of Jesus. Household enemies are the most dangerous. Another African proverb says, *"If you do not die at home,(i.e. being killed) you are not likely to die outside."* Why is that? Your home folks know everything about you; they listen to your dreams, testimonies, ambitions and visions. They are unavoidable; blood ties are not easily cut off. Abel could not escape the wickedness of Cain. A kiss from a close friend could be a signal for an arrest and death.. Jacob narrowly escaped untimely death from his blood brother Esau. Isaac faced the greatest challenge of his life from Ishmael. Who else had the power to delay the destiny of Abraham other than Lot? Achan a man trusted by Joshua, to be one of his fighters separated him from the promise of God at the battle of Ai. (Joshua 7:20-21) That of Joseph was more complex because ten of his brothers agreed and plotted to kill him. They wanted to stop the will of God in Joseph's life.

Truly, no one can stop the will of God for you, but it can be unduly delayed. We don't know for how long we have delayed the coming of our Lord Jesus through our nonchalant attitude to the spreading of the gospel. It is the responsibility of every believer to resist Satan in every way possible. Matthew 11:12 *"And from the days of*

John the Baptist until now the kingdom of heaven suffers violence, and the violent take it by force." You will have to obtain your right forcefully in the place of prayer and take the steps of faith.

Gen 37:17- 28 " So Joseph went after his brothers and found them in Dothan. 18 Now when they saw him afar off, even before he came near them, they conspired against him to kill him. 19 Then they said to one another, "Look, this dreamer is coming! 20 Come therefore, let us now kill him and cast him into some pit; and we shall say, 'Some wild beast has devoured him.' We shall see what will become of his dreams!" 21 But Reuben heard it, and he delivered him out of their hands, and said, "Let us not kill him." 22 And Reuben said to them, "Shed no blood, but cast him into this pit which is in the wilderness, and do not lay a hand on him"-that he might deliver him out of their hands, and bring him back to his father. 23 So it came to pass, when Joseph had come to his brothers, that they stripped Joseph of his tunic, the tunic of many colors that was on him. 24 Then they took him and cast him into a pit. And the pit was empty; there was no water in it. 25 And they sat down to eat a meal. Then they lifted their eyes and looked, and there was a company of Ishmaelites, coming from Gilead with their camels, bearing spices, balm, and myrrh, on their way to carry them down to Egypt. 26 So Judah said to his brothers, "What profit is there if we kill our brother and conceal his blood? 27 Come and let us sell him to the Ishmaelites, and let not our hand be upon him, for he is our brother and our flesh." And his brothers listened. 28 Then Midianite traders passed by; so the brothers pulled Joseph up and lifted him out of the pit, and sold him to the Ishmaelites for twenty shekels of silver. And they took Joseph to Egypt".

Dothan means law or custom, while *Shechem* means "early in the morning". Joseph was sent out early in the morning of his life by the custom of obedience to parental orders; the enemy waited to take his life, terminate his dream and put asunder the agenda of a divine providence. Joseph was not only a comforter to the tribe of Israel; he was a comforter to the whole world. He was a type of Christ. The seed of wisdom placed in him by the Porter was supposed to save the nation of Egypt from a devastating famine. Household enemies place more threat and danger to the world than the arsenals of Pentagon or any weapon of super power nations. What would have happened to the Gentiles in kingdom matters if Paul's life was not divinely preserved? What would the world have looked like if envious family members had killed great inventors in science and technology? Divine favor showed up for Joseph and there was a division among his brothers. Reuben could no longer consent to the killing of his brother. Judah was used by God to deliver him (Joseph) from death by suffocation in an empty well. This action set Joseph on the road to Egypt where he ruled according to the mind of God as revealed to Abraham in

Genesis 15:12-16. 12 Now when the sun was going down, a deep sleep fell upon Abram; and behold, horror and great darkness fell upon him. 13 Then He said to Abram: "Know certainly that your descendants will be strangers in a land that is not theirs, and will serve them, and they will afflict them four hundred years. 14 And also the nation whom they serve will judge; afterward they shall

25

come out with great possessions. 15 Now as for you, you shall go to your fathers in peace; you shall be buried at a good old age. 16 But in the fourth generation they shall return here, for the iniquity of the Amorites is not yet complete."

Household enemies are always so formidable because of the amount of evidence and information at their disposal. They cannot be pleased, they will always find a fault to justify an act of wickedness. All the efforts of David to please Saul proved abortive. Gentiles were not the people that crucified Jesus but fellow sons of Abraham. Only the God of Abraham, Isaac and Jacob can deliver you from the enemies among family members or very close associates through the divine favor called the *Blood of Jesus.* Who could have saved Joseph from ten envious brothers, but God? No wisdom of man can deliver someone hated by his family members. They may not kill, but they can sell you into slavery. I have interviewed a lot of people, especially Africans in America who have sworn never to go back to their homelands because of fear of household wickedness. Jesus was taken out of Israel to Egypt by a divine order to escape death from household wickedness. According to Matt.2: 19- 20 *" Now when they had departed, behold, an angel of the Lord appeared to Joseph in a dream, saying, "Arise, take the young Child and His mother, flee to Egypt, and stay there until I bring you word; for Herod will seek the young Child to destroy Him."* You need the hand of God to escape the plots of household enemies.

Pray these prayers very aggressively:

1. Father of my Lord Jesus Christ, set me free from my household enemies, in Jesus name.
2. Everyone that has been given the role to be my shepherd, do not be deaf to divine orders to preserve my life in Jesus name.
3. O Lord, grant me the ability to obey you in Jesus name.
4. O God of Joseph, hide my destiny from every stargazer, witches, and wizards in Jesus' name.
5. O Lord, deliver me from the enemies that act like friends in the name of Jesus.
6. O Lord, let no one have access to my destiny in Jesus name.
7. O God, transform me to fire that can never be quenched in the name of Jesus.
8. Oh God, if there is any evil (mention: poverty, sickness, untimely death) in my destiny, change it today in the name of Jesus.
9. If there is a covenant between me and the operators of powers of darkness, break that covenant today in the name of Jesus.
10. Jehovah Nissi, wage war against every power opposing my greatness in the name of Jesus.

Chapter Four

Divine Errors

$\mathcal{T}$he word of God from Genesis to Revelation is full of divine errors. A divine error in this context will be defined as the will of God executed on behalf of a servant of God by his enemy. That is, everything that the enemy meant for evil, God turned it to good. The crucifixion of our LORD Jesus was a divine error orchestrated by God Himself - *1 Cor.2:8 " which none of the rulers of this age knew; for had they known, they would not have crucified the Lord of glory"*

The way God chose to purchase salvation for humanity was to shed the blood of His son, so He could receive Him to His right hand in Heaven. The wicked people that crucified Jesus Christ committed a divine error. If they had known that the death of Jesus on the cross would lead to their spiritual death and loss of the authority that was taken away from Adam through deception, they would not have done it. In like manner the brothers of Joseph killed a goat and used its blood to soak his coat so they could deceive Jacob their father. The blood they shed was a divine sacrifice needed for Joseph to overcome the powers of the enemy that rose up against him, which is a type of the blood of Jesus that eventually erased old identities. His enemies were no longer able to recognize him (2 Cor. 5:17) It caused his light to shine and darkness was not able to comprehend it (John 1:5-7). It protected him from the destiny destroyer. (Gal 6:17). The sacrifice was made to the detriment of his enemies. The identity of man was replaced by a divine identity. Man became a *"new creature"* as his brothers could no longer recognize him (Joseph). *Gen.42:8* <u>*So Joseph*</u> <u>*recognized his brothers, but they did not recognize him.*</u> *9 Then Joseph remembered the dreams which he had dreamed about them,*

The power to escape from the enemy that you cannot run away from, is found only in the blood. As Joseph's brothers killed the goat and soaked his coat in it, the final price was paid to establish his dream. At that point in the life of Joseph, no weapon fashioned against him could prosper. And the tongue of Portiphar's wife" that would rise up against him was already condemned because he later obtained an heritage in the blood of the Lamb. No nation or individual without the blood can reach his or her full potential in life. Jesus said in John 15:5 *"I am the vine, you are the branches. He who abides in **me**, and I in him, bears much fruit; for without me you can do nothing."* Nations and people not redeemed by the blood are rising to total destruction. Do your enemies have the information about your old self; are familiar with your coat of many colors? On the day of your salvation, the coat was totally soaked in the blood, and it can never regain its original state.

Take note, bloodstain is indelible! Satan can never recover from the regrets of his mistake.

Thank God for the afflictions (if any) that led you to Christ. It was a divine error for Satan. If he had known; you would not have been persuaded to giving your life to Jesus Christ. If you have not yet given your life to Him, pause now. Ask Him (Jesus Christ) to save your soul and wash you with His blood. The blood will make you to recognize your enemies but will not allow them to recognize you. Afflictions will not come a second time, upon you. Now your cup can even run over in the presence of your enemies. Jesus promised to save you and your household, so do not wish them dead. Pray for their salvation also. Whatever they meant for evil God will turn it to good.

The actions of your enemies will lead you to your destiny. The enemies of the cross led Jesus Christ of Nazareth to the right hand side of God the Father. The only achievement of your enemy is to push you to your 'Portiphar's house'. This will only end up in preparing you for the life and culture of the palace. David was trained in the palace of Saul. Every born-again Christian is preparing for a life in the palace, John 14:1-3. Only those who sleep with Portiphar's wife (i.e, those who compromise) will never get to live in the same mansions with the King of Kings. God was with Joseph, so he did not compromise, like Jesus who said in John 14:30 *"for the ruler of this world is coming, and he has nothing in Me"*.

Pray aggressively and say aloud the following prayer points.

1. After the order of Joseph and other children of Israel; I erase every satanic identity in my life with the blood of Jesus.
2. Let my life become so precious in the sight of every one too powerful for me in the name of Jesus.
3. Let there be a major division in the camp of my enemies in the name of Jesus.
4. O Lord, use my enemies to propel me to my land of promise in Jesus name.
5. O Lord, let me enjoy your presence at every stage of my life in the name of Jesus.
6. Turn every fire of affliction to an air condition environment for me in the name of Jesus Christ.
7. Let my enemies lack the ability to recognize me in the name of Jesus Christ.
8. I decree restoration to my divine dreams and passions in the name of Jesus Christ.
9. O God, my Creator, let my cup of joy overflow in the presence of my enemies in the name of Jesus Christ.
10. I shall have dominion over every issues of life at any point of my life in the name of Jesus.

Chapter Five

Enemies At The Market Place

The first market place experience of Joseph was working as a slave in Potiphar's house. The account of his sojourn in Egypt and the favor of God upon his life are found in scripture below.

Genesis 39:1-23 "Now Joseph had been taken down to Egypt. And Potiphar, an officer of Pharaoh, captain of the guard, an Egyptian, bought him from the Ishmaelites who had taken him down there. 2 The LORD was with Joseph, and he was a successful man; and he was in the house of his master the Egyptian. 3 And his master saw that the LORD was with him and that the LORD made all he did to prosper in his hand. 4 So Joseph found favor in his sight, and served him. Then he made him overseer of his house, and all that he had he put under his authority. 5 So it was, from the time that he had made him overseer of his house and all that he had, that the LORD blessed the Egyptian's house for Joseph's sake; and the blessing of the LORD was on all that he had in the house and in the field. 6 Thus he left all that he had in Joseph's hand, and he did not know what he had except for the bread, which he ate. Now Joseph was handsome in form and appearance. *7 And it came to pass after these things that his master's wife cast longing eyes on Joseph, and she said, "Lie with me."* *8 But he refused and said to his master's wife, "Look, my master does not know what is with me in the house, and he* has committed all that he has to my hand. *9 There is no one greater in this house than I, nor has he kept back anything from me but you, because you are his wife. How then can I do this great wickedness, and sin against God?"* *10 So it was, as she spoke to Joseph day by day, that he did not heed her, to lie with her or to be with her.* *11 But it happened about this time, when Joseph went into the house to do his work, and none of the men of the house was inside, 12 that she caught him by his garment, saying, "Lie with me." But he left his garment in her hand, and fled and ran outside. 13 And so it was, when she saw that he had left his garment in her hand and fled outside, 14 that she called to the men of her house and spoke to them, saying, "See, he has brought in to us a Hebrew to mock us. He came in to me to lie with me, and I cried out with a loud voice. 15 And it happened, when he heard that I lifted my voice and cried out, that he left his garment with me, and fled and went outside." 16 So she kept his garment with her until his master came home. 17 Then she spoke to him with words like these, saying, "The Hebrew servant whom you brought to us came in to me to mock me; 18 so it happened, as I lifted my voice and cried out, that he left his garment with me and fled outside." 19 So it was, when his master heard the words which his wife spoke to him, saying, "Your servant did to me after this manner," that his anger was aroused. 20 Then Joseph's master took him and put him into the prison, a place where the king's prisoners were confined. And he was there in the prison. 21 But the LORD was with Joseph and showed him mercy, and He gave him favor in the sight of the keeper of the prison. 22 And the keeper of the prison committed to Joseph's hand all the prisoners who were in the prison; whatever they did there, it was his doing. 23 The keeper of the prison did not look into anything that was under*

Joseph's authority,[c] because the LORD was with him; and whatever he did, the LORD made it prosper."

A slave does not receive wages; he has already been bought with a price, thus, he must serve his master(s) all the days of his life. This again is the type of the life Jesus lived on earth, to serve the will of the Father. He took no credit to himself but to the Father who sent Him. Joseph had no other option but to serve his master because he was a slave. His coat of many colors which reminded him of his heritage, had been baptized in the blood; he had been humbled to be content with a life of hard work without wages. He had lost his identity, his father Jacob was no longer there for him.; literarily, he was down to the lowest ebb of his life at that time. He was now subject to a life of servitude in Egypt for the rest of his life. According to the words of a 1684 songwriter John Bunyan:

> *He that is down needs fear no fall,*
> *he that is low no pride;*
> *he that is humble ever shall*
> *have God to be his guide.*
> *I am content with what I have*
> *little be it or much;*
> *and, Lord, contentment still I crave,*
> *because thou savest such.*

All objects of pride had been removed from Joseph; his only solace was to serve Potiphar and his household with humility and obedience. Joseph chose to be diligent in all that he did. From the above passage, we could see that the presence of God is independent of space or place. Once the blood has removed a satanic identity, Jesus will never leave you nor forsake you. Joseph had the boldness to say 'NO' to satanic advances. The boldness to speak the truth came upon the apostles on the day of Pentecost in (Act.2:1-9). and they never compromised after that day. Threats of death or prison did not let them deny Jesus.

Satan is a liar and the father of all lies. Any lie told against a righteous person is only a catalyst to a major breakthrough. From the passage, the fear of God will not allow Joseph to compromise his belief, but the lie of Potiphar's wife set the stage for him to meet people who eventually led him to the palace. There was no account that Joseph was homesick, but the children of Israel were homesick in the wilderness, they were thinking of the cucumber of Egypt, but not the power that set them free from Pharaoh. This led to untold hardships. A river that forgets its source, it is said, soon becomes dry. Joseph did not forget his God, but he forgot about the past evils of his brothers. He focused on his new assignment and the fear of God that delivered him from his envious brothers.

No liars or backsliders can enjoy the full loyalty of Jehovah. Joseph was doing his job very faithfully and God prospered the works of his hand. The house of

Potiphar became very prosperous. Potiphar made him the chief administrator of his house. He was very diligent he would not go beyond his bounds. The greatest favor of God over the life of any man is the presence of God. If God be for us who can be against us, but the greatest of all is for you to know that God is with you. The bible says, *"my people perish for lack of knowledge"*. You must be sure He is with you before you can enjoy His presence. Satan entered into the heart of Potiphar's wife, and she lusted after her slave. The lady that was his boss' wife, a woman who could have been his mentor or mother in a strange land, degenerated to such a low position of a youth seducer! Obviously, Satan had replaced her dignity and self-respect with shamelessness. Most Christians today will see Portiphar's wife's love advance as a genuine excuse to sin. He did not initiate the move. She did! But Joseph realized that he would not only be committing sin against his master, but he also against God Almighty. Though young, Joseph saw this as an attack on his destiny at his place of work. There are many men of God or (Pastors) who are supposed to be shepherds to their sheep, but have rather committed fornication or adultery with them, at the flimsiest excuse of loneliness. Directors of companies have destroyed many destinies as a result of demonic affections.

The reason why God brought Joseph to Egypt was much bigger than Portiphar's house. It was the beginning of the fulfillment of the prophecy that was delivered unto

Abraham concerning his children in Egypt. God had promised, they would leave Egypt with great stuff. Where were they going to find the great stuff if they will be destroyed by famine? God who knows the beginning from the end was starting all over what Satan had destroyed in the Garden of Eden. Man was created to have dominion. Joseph knew he was created to exemplify the dominion that had been covenanted to man. Family ties, good credit, clear criminal record or whatever man has put as hindrances cannot stop the execution of that dominion by God.

According to Apostle Paul in the book of Romans: Rom.3: 3-4 *"for what if some did not believe? Will their unbelief make the faithfulness of God without effect? Certainly not! Indeed, let God be true but every man a liar."*

Moses allowed anger to prevent him from reaching the Promised Land. Depression and fear cut short the destiny of Elijah. According to Joshua 13:1, God was not totally pleased with Joshua. There were many lands still left for him to possess. People like Achan (Joshua 7:1) in his camp had contributed to slowing him down.

Joseph was a type of Jesus, in terms of his life - He finished the race set before him. Every aspect of his dreams was fulfilled. The sun, the moon and the eleven stars bowed down to him. People of other nations also bowed down to Joseph as they came to buy food in

Egypt. Joseph exhibited the earthly dominion. The heaven and the earth were in agreement with him. There was no record of any malpractice or lack of authority in Joseph.

Genesis 47:18: *When that year was ended, they came unto him the second year, and said unto him, We will not hide it from my lord, how that our money is spent; my lord also hath our herds of cattle; there is not ought left in the sight of my lord, but our bodies, and our lands: 19 Wherefore shall we die before thine eyes, both we and our land? buy us and our land for bread, and we and our land will be servants unto Pharaoh: and give us seed, that we may live, and not die, that the land be not desolate.*

Joseph indeed finished the race as every aspects of his dream were established. It is good to ask the question, - What was the favor that delivered him from the hand of his master's wife? The answer is found in Gen.39:8 *But he refused and said to his master's wife, "Look, my master does not know what is with me in the house, and he has committed all that he has to my hand. 9 There is no one greater in this house than I, nor has he kept back anything from me but you, because you are his wife. How then can I do this great wickedness, and sin against God?"* Joseph considered any act of immorality as a sin against God. This statement gave an insight into the heart of Joseph. He knew that any favor he had ever received was from no man, but from God. He did not make any reference to his father's dignity and love nor his master that had entrusted him with all things. There are many people who have ended their life's journey in the house of Portiphar (sin).

Consider David the King after he committed adultery with Bathsheba. He acknowledged his sin as not only against Uriah or any other in Israel, but against God as we read in Psalm 51. David was able to receive God's mercy because of his repentant and humble heart. The throne of David was therefore not only divinely established, but was covenanted to be forever.

There are some believers who are brazenly sleeping with their master's wives. They even speak and walk like the master. Sleeping with Portiphar's wife is to compromise the standards of God. The bible said concerning these group of believers at the last day in Matt.7:21-23

Not everyone who says to me, 'Lord, Lord,' shall enter the kingdom of heaven, but he who does the will of My Father in heaven. 22 Many will say to Me in that day, 'Lord, Lord, have we not prophesied in Your name, cast out demons in Your name, and done many wonders in Your name?' 23 And then I will declare to them, 'I never knew you; depart from Me, you who practice lawlessness!

Reaching the full potential of your dream demands total understanding of God's ways. The life of Joseph was pleasing to God. Prov. 16:7 says, *"When a man's ways please the LORD, he maketh even his enemies to be at peace with him"* As a slave in a foreign land, and with the exalted position of Portiphar, Joseph's life could have been taken without anyone asking any questions. We read several times. *"...but God was with Joseph"* God was so personal to Joseph and he knew it. He would not lose those dreams for anything!

God is tired of people who are destined to become Medical Doctors but became complacent when they obtained only a RN (Registered Nurse) license. God is not happy with people who are destined to become billionaires but get comfortable in their jobs earning meagre wages. Some have had dreams of becoming President, Governor, or Business Tycoons, but as soon as they get to "Portiphar's house" (comfort zone) they give up on their dreams.

How disastrous it would have been for the present day Christians if Apostle Peter had followed after the multitude of fish he caught when Jesus entered his boat. Peter chose to be a fisher of men instead for something of less value What would have happened if Apostle Paul had stopped where Peter also stopped? Gentiles would have been prevented from the benefits of the Holy Spirit-led lifestyle.

What height have you attained in your chosen career or your walk with God? There is still room at the top! Peter's shadow was said to cast out demons, while the aprons from Paul was working wonders. In any area of life God has placed us, He expects our integrity and the fear of God to sustain us whenever we are caught in the web of sin, no matter how attractive it may be. Israel suffered greatly when Samson fell at the lap of Delilah. Judges 16:1-19. You must not end your life while you are still under training for the life in the palace. The utmost place is for power to change hands. Pharaoh must give you his ring and signet. The scripture says, the wealth of the Gentiles is laid up for the just. Don't settle for less. The dominion power promised by God in Gen.1:28, is yours for the asking.

Isaiah 60:5, &11

*"Then you shall see and become radiant, And your heart shall swell with joy; Because the abundance of the sea shall be turned to you, The **wealth** of the Gentiles shall come to you. Therefore your gates shall be open continually; They shall not be shut day or night, That men may bring to you the **wealth** of the Gentiles, And their kings in procession"*

Pray the following prayers aloud and aggressively:

1. Enemies at the market place of my life receive judgment in the name of Jesus.
2. Spirit of temporary comfort, I rebuke you in the name of Jesus.
3. Powers assigned to limit growth, I judged you with the blood of Jesus.

4. Powers that will separate me from divine mercy, receive terminal judgment in the name of Jesus.
5. I divorce myself from any alliance with the haters of my destiny.
6. Holy Ghost fire; propel me to my land of covenant in the name of Jesus.
7. I command the archangels of the Most High God to remove every road blocks to the total fulfillment of my dreams in the name of Jesus.
8. Powers against my gainful employment, I come against you in the name of Jesus.
9. All attempts wicked people at my place of work will lead to my promotion in the name of Jesus.
10. I receive the grace to meditate on the word of God everyday of my life, so I can have good success in the name of Jesus.

Chapter Six

The Turning Point

*B*efore you get to the place of your dream, you must be ready to interpret the dream of others. Henry Ford of America interpreted a giant dream in an automobile industry that later gave birth to Ford Motors. Bill Gates interpreted dreams that have created jobs, businesses and wealth for uncountable individuals in the computer industry. You must interpret the dreams of others before you can get to your land of promise. It is easier to interpret dream for kings, but you must be ready to interpret the dreams of prisoners while you are also in the prison. It is great to pastor rich and influential people; but you must be ready to pastor the poor and homeless people on the streets. The way up is down, the number of people you can help to smile is always proportional to the amount of joy that will come your way. The bible promises the fullness of joy, only to those who are ready to interpret the dream of others. According to Zig Zigler, in his book, *See You At The Top,* he wrote " *You can get everything in life you want if you help enough other people get what they want.*"

Joseph was a Crown Prince in the house of Jacob, yet God sent unbelievable people his way. He had all the right to have an attitude in the house of Portiphar. He would not have make it to the point of envy if he did not excel in washing toilets, washing clothes, undergarments and all dirty jobs reserved only for slaves. If that was a coincidence, would he have become Chief of Prisoners, assigned to special prisoners like the baker and the Butler if he was not a diligent prisoner? Although Jesus was God, He humbled Himself. He had to live a life of service. Washing the apostles' feet and taking insults from the people he came to save

Gen. 40: 7-19: 7 So he asked Pharaoh's officers who were with him in the custody of his lord's house, saying, "Why do you look so sad today?" 8 And they said to him, "We each have had a dream, and there is no interpreter of it." So Joseph said to them, "Do not interpretations belong to God? Tell them to me, please." 9 Then the chief butler told his dream to Joseph, and said to him, "Behold, in my dream a vine was before me, 10 and in the vine were three branches; it was as though it budded, its blossoms shot forth, and its clusters brought forth ripe grapes. 11 Then Pharaoh's cup was in my hand; and I took the grapes and pressed them into Pharaoh's cup, and placed the cup in Pharaoh's hand." 12 And Joseph said to him, "This is the interpretation of it: The three branches are three days. 13 Now within three days Pharaoh will lift up your head and restore you to your place, and you will put Pharaoh's cup in his hand according to the former manner, when you were his butler. 14 But remember me when it is well with you, and please show kindness to me; make mention of me to Pharaoh, and get me out of this house. 15 For indeed I was stolen away from the land of the Hebrews; and also I have done nothing here that they should put me into the dungeon.” 16 When the chief baker saw that the interpretation was good, he said to Joseph, “I also was in my dream, and there were three white baskets on my head. 17 In the uppermost basket were all kinds of baked goods for Pharaoh, and the birds ate them out of the basket on my head.” 18 So Joseph answered and said, “This is the interpretation of it: The three baskets are three days. 19 Within three days Pharaoh will lift off your head from you and hang you on a tree; and the birds will eat your flesh from you.”

Pride and over-confidence have prevented so many people from getting to the place of their dreams. It is true God has spoken to you; It is true the power of God is moving in your life, but the place God is taking you to is so big, only God can take you there. You cannot plan your way there; you cannot even see it in your dream. What you have seen is a parable; your little mind cannot figure it out. God is able to exceed your expectations. Be diligent in your "Portiphar's house" and in the Egyptian prison. God that promised to reward diligence will connect you to your "Pharaoh" who will be willing to relinquish to you all the power you need to live your dream in the name of Jesus. Joseph had the opportunity to interpret the dream of Pharaoh.

Gen. 41 ; 37-44 So the advice was good in the eyes of Pharaoh and in the eyes of all his servants. 38 And Pharaoh said to his servants, “Can we find such a one as this, a man in whom is the Spirit of God?” 39 Then Pharaoh said to Joseph, “Inasmuch as God has shown you all this, there is no one as discerning and wise as you. 40 You shall be over my house, and all my people shall be ruled according to your word; only in regard to the throne will I be greater than you." 41 And Pharaoh said to Joseph, "See, I have set you over all the land of Egypt." 42 Then Pharaoh took his signet ring off his hand and put it on Joseph's hand; and he clothed him in garments of fine linen and put a gold chain around his neck. 43 And he had him ride in the second chariot, which he had; and they cried out before him, "Bow the knee!" So he set him over all the land of Egypt. 44 Pharaoh also said to Joseph, "I am Pharaoh, and without your consent no man may lift his hand or foot in all the land of Egypt."

Joseph was given the opportunity to use his talent, which he had put to work in the prison. A talent when put to work becomes a skill. Skill well utilized takes people to their dream. God the giver of dreams will always give opportunities that will translate your dream to reality. Every system of the enemy put in place in your life to frustrate the agenda of heaven for your life shall be destroyed in the name of Jesus.

Joseph's advice was good in the presence of someone that has power to promote him; I speak to the life of every reader that your advice will attract a dividend beyond your expectations in the name of Jesus. Please pray these prayers very aggressively.

1. Every demonic impartation on my life waiting for manifestation at my turning point, receive divine destruction in the name of Jesus.

2. All anti success invocations programmed into my future I command the virus of God to corrupt you completely in the name of Jesus.
3. I block my hearing to all demonic auto-suggestions in the name of Jesus.
4. You spirit that promotes selfish agenda inside of me, I put you under control in the name of Jesus.
5. After the order of Joseph and Daniel, my dreams will not die until I interpret the dreams of others in Jesus name.
6. O Lord, perfume my life with favor in Jesus name.
7. I expunge every quitter's mentality from my life, I will not quit at the edge of my miracle in the name of Jesus.

Chapter Seven

Staying At The Top.

It is better not to have been a champion than to be an ex-champion. The life of Samson (Judges 16) was a pathetic story of someone who could not stay on top throughout his tenure. Power left him when he needed it the most. Getting a job is not always as difficult as keeping it. The story of Joseph after he had been promoted to the highest position possible in the land as narrated in the passage below.

Genesis 45: *So no one stood with him while Joseph made himself known to his brothers. 2 And he wept aloud, and the Egyptians and the house of Pharaoh heard it. 3 Then Joseph said to his brothers, "I am Joseph; does my father still live?" But his brothers could not answer him, for they were dismayed in his presence. 4 And Joseph said to his brothers, "Please come near to me." So they came near. Then he said: "I am Joseph your brother, whom you sold into Egypt. 5 But now. 6 For these two years the famine has been in the land, and there are still five years in which there will be neither plowing nor harvesting. 7 And God sent me before you to preserve posterity for you in the earth, and to save your lives by a great deliverance. 8 So now it was not you who sent me here, but God; and He has made me a father to Pharaoh, and lord of all his house, and a ruler throughout all the land of Egypt. 9 "Hurry and go up to my father, and say to him, 'Thus says your son Joseph: "God has made me lord of all Egypt; come down to me, do not tarry. 10 You shall dwell in the land of Goshen, and you shall be near to me, you and your children, your children's children, your flocks and your herds, and all that you have. 11 There I will provide for you, lest you and your household, and all that you have, come to poverty; for there are still five years of famine."' 12 "And behold, your eyes and the eyes of my brother Benjamin see that it is my mouth that speaks to you. 13 So you shall tell my father of all my glory in Egypt, and of all that you have seen; and you shall hurry and bring my father down here." 14 Then he fell on his brother Benjamin's neck and wept, and Benjamin wept on his neck. 15 Moreover he kissed all his brothers and wept over them, and after that his brothers talked with him. 16 Now the report of it was heard in Pharaoh's house, saying, "Joseph's brothers have come." So it pleased Pharaoh and his servants well. 17 And Pharaoh said to Joseph, "Say to your brothers, 'Do this: Load your animals and depart; go to the land of Canaan. 18 Bring your father and your households and come to me; I will give you the best of the land of Egypt, and you will eat the fat of the land. 19 Now you are commanded-do this: Take carts out of the land of Egypt for your little ones and your wives; bring your father and come. 20 Also do not be concerned about your goods, for the best of all the land of Egypt is yours.'" 21 Then the sons of Israel did so; and Joseph gave them carts, according to the command of Pharaoh, and he gave them provisions for the journey.*

The strength that takes people up is far less than the strength that sustains them there. I have seen many people that have set goals to loose weight and have achieved their goals. It is however sad to note that few people keep up with the new weight attained. If millions of people who surrendered their lives to Jesus at Billy

Graham's crusades remained committed to the faith, the result would be tremendous.

It took only twelve apostles of Jesus to help us to welcome the gospel. They were described as people who turned the world upside down. Making money is not as difficult as maintaining the riches. Samson was born with the anointing; he however could not keep it to the end. David almost blew it, if not for the mercy of God. Joseph our case study like Jesus did not allow the fame of Egypt to enter his head. There are a few lessons to be learnt from the above passage. There is no question in my heart that you will get to the top after reading and using this book. You will get to the top and remain at the top in the name of Jesus

1. Joseph made himself known to his brothers.

A river that forgets its source will surely dry up. The promise of God is to save you and your household. Do not forget your roots; make yourself known. The power that brought you to the top is able to sustain you. Do not undermine the power through your own fears. Most people that Jesus healed were sent back to their relatives as testimony of the unlimited powers of God. Make yourself known; do not hide the great testimony. It is from the Lord.

2.   He wept aloud

He sobbed uncontrollably, reminding himself of the mercy and grace of God that preserved his life. He was humbled; there was neither strength nor pride in him. To stay at the top you must be able to think so deeply about how you got to the top. Your brokenness must be transparent. He wept aloud and the Egyptians heard him. Though now a king, the attitude of a child who is always responsive to a father's directives was still seen in him. Humility is the watchword that keeps leaders in charge.

3.   He remembered his first love

He asked, does my father still live?" He asked about the father that loved him. Jesus made every sacrifice through fasting, service, and pains, to please the father who gave Him all the power. He was in contact, expressing words and deeds of love and affections. Joseph asked after the welfare of his father whom he had not seen or talked to in thirteen years!

To remain at the top, you must not forget your first love. Don't forget people that made it possible for you to be where you are today. The word of God in Revelation 2:4 says, *"Nevertheless I have this against you, that you have left your first love" Do not forget your first love"*

4. Be a blessing to your relatives

Joseph said to his brothers *"Please come near to me"* This is a great lesson for those who want to remain on top. Do not despise your root. You were not blessed to be a reproach to your heritage. The fact that he was a governor in Egypt does not make him an Egyptian. When the level of his success intimidated his brothers, he begged them to come close. Jesus after resurrection took no offence; He went back to his people, identified with them, ate fish with them, and broke bread with them. He allowed the doubting Thomas to touch him. Do not separate yourself from the people for which reason you were blessed.

5. Have a forgiving spirit

Joseph said, *"do not therefore be grieved or angry with yourselves because you sold me here; for God sent me before you to preserve life"* There is always anger and grief in the life of the wicked; only the spirit of forgiveness can bring out the will of God. Jesus prayed for those who hurt him, and this was the secret of His power.

Luke 23:34 *"Jesus said, Father, forgive them; for they know not what they do".*

Make excuses for your enemies, God used them to prepare you for the place of your dream. **It is not**

possible to be a blessing to a people you are not ready to forgive. The act of forgiveness activates divine favors from God, and this manifests in uncommon wisdom, power and glory needed to stay at the top.

6.   Obey the law of the land that offers you the opportunity.

As Joseph was diligent in the house of Portiphar and in the prison, so he was as a Governor. He obeyed the rules of Egypt, so Pharaoh loved him. No leader loves an assistant that has no respect for him. Joseph as a prisoner could be made to do what he was doing without adequate or any compensation. Jesus also paid taxes to Caesar and obeyed constituted authority. Only a law-abiding leader will remain on top as long as they live.

7. Honor your vows.

Joseph honored his vows to his father. He took good care of his brothers while Israel was living and after his death. He buried his father according to the instruction Israel left behind, and never revenged any unrighteousness committed against him. Integrity is not in eye service but commitment to our spoken words. Your word is you, sooner or later; a leader that cannot keep to their words will loose credibility.

Pray aggressively as follows with a loud voice:

1. Give me a blessing that overcome every form of fear in Jesus name.
2. Give me a breakthrough that will force all enemies at the root to bow down to me. in the name of Jesus.
3. Oh Lord as you helped Jacob to overcome the fear of Esau, help me in the name of Jesus.
4. I reject every wealth that will eventually destroy my life in the name of Jesus.
5. Father in the name of Jesus; grant me success that will keep me close to you.
6. Give me a name that will be closely associated with your name in the name of Jesus.
7. I divorce myself from every form of poverty, in the name of Jesus.
8. Let my pharaoh be willing to surrender his throne unto me in the name of Jesus.
9. Oh God of Joseph, let me have an answer for all tempters of my life in Jesus name..
10. Father in the name of Jesus; keep every organs of my body under your merciful control.
11. I shall not die with my music still in me, in the name of Jesus.
12. Holy Spirit, saturate me with wisdom to attract unlimited wealth in the name of Jesus.
13. Father let all forces under heaven assist me to prosper beyond all I can think or imagine in the name of Jesus.

14. Begin to thank God for answer prayers.

Chapter Eight

Breakthrough Prayer

Jesus said in Matt.7:7 *"Ask and it shall be given unto you..."* Please before you proceed on these prayers, if you have not surrendered your life to Jesus, Do it now, if you are not sure you are a child of God or you have been having challenges for living a life of holiness and righteousness; please re-dedicate your life to Jesus Christ. The bible says in Acts 3:19 *"Repent and be converted, then your sins will be blotted out..."* After dedication or re-dedication you must discard anything in your possession that has demonic origin.

When I became born-again and gave up the Islamic religion, I discarded every paraphernalia that identified me as a Muslim. I am now proud to be called a Christian. I thank God for all those who prayed for my conversion. It is indeed a breakthrough.

"If any man be in Christ, is a new creature, old things are passed away, behold all things become new" 2 Cor.5:17.

When I was a Muslim and practiced African fetish beliefs, I used to recite some prayers, over and over again. I labored in search of peace for my soul and freedom from demonic oppression. I never knew there is a name freely given to every man or woman that will sustain a willing and believing soul in freedom from all powers of darkness. Today, I am a testimony, I have access to the name of Jesus and the power of God through the Holy Spirit who helps me with break-through prayers, some of which I have put down for you. Pray them and be blessed.

The newness of the Holy Spirit as evidenced in the life of Saul of Tarsus, who became Apostle Paul and all other saints who genuinely surrendered their lives to Jesus will be your portion also in the name of Jesus; Amen.

Pray the following prayers and very aggressively with all your heart.

1. My Lord and my maker, my Savior and Redeemer the lover of my soul, I recognize your authority over my life. You gave me life and you are the only one who can take it from me. I give you praise. You are the author and finisher of my faith, I worship you. There is no one like you. You are higher than the highest. Taller than the tallest, bigger than the biggest, without you there is no other. Heaven is your throne, the earth is your foot stool, all power, and all honor and glory originate from you. Your son

Jesus was the lamb you sacrificed to pay for my sins. The sacrifice of your only son set me free from all powers, thrones and dominions that have made covenant to separate me from your love. I praise you; I give you all the glory because of who you are. Faithful father I will love you for ever, because you first loved me. You did not allow the pregnancy that brought me to life to be aborted. You did not allow the mistakes of my parents to cut my life short. You are beautiful beyond description. Your love for me is beyond description, you are the Almighty God, nothing is impossible with you. You are the covenant of Abraham, the joy of Sarah, fruitfulness of Isaac, beauty of Esther, courage of Daniel and the testimony of Paul. You are awesome, You are worthy, You are faithful. My love for you is not a lie. I give you praise, I honor you. Please accept my praise in the name of Jesus.

2. Father in the name of Jesus, I ask for forgiveness for every sin of disobedience I have ever committed. In every way I have disobeyed you, please forgive me. Save my soul from eternal destruction, write my name in the book of life.

3. Father in the name of Jesus remind me of every anti-progress habits that have been limiting my success and grant me the courage to forsake them.

4. Father every doorway that the enemy is using to enter into my life; I decree them closed in the name

of Jesus. I divorce myself from every relationship that is limiting my love for my maker, in the name of Jesus.

5. I resign from every assignment that supports and promotes the works of darkness in the name of Jesus.

6. Father, grant me the grace to say NO to every evil task masters anytime they come to me, whether physically or spiritually in the name of Jesus.

7. Great Porter and the creator of the universe, grant me freedom from every forms of oppression in the name of Jesus.

8. O God of Abraham, Isaac and Jacob, establish me in your righteousness, let me be far away from oppression in the name of Jesus.

9. Father annul any election voted against my destiny no matter how free and fair it may appear in the name of Jesus.

10. Oh, God! Disregard and destroy any covenant made with death by anyone to frustrate my destiny in the name of Jesus.

11. Father, I decree in the name of Jesus, any agreement made with the grave by anyone living or dead against my destiny is hereby cancelled and all its negative impact reversed now in Jesus name.

12. O Lord, let the wind of the Holy Spirit sweep away every refuge of lies against my life in the name of Jesus.

13. I switch on the light of the Holy Spirit upon my life in the name of Jesus.

14. I activate the spirit of discernments and the grace for total obedience to the voice of God in the name of Jesus.
15. I activate the ability of my heart to conceive divine ideas in the name of Jesus.
16. I surrender myself to the instructions of heavenly teachers in the name of Jesus.
17. Father I surrender my body to the full operation of heavenly mechanic upon my body for a complete tune up and regular maintenance in the name of Jesus.
18. I surrender every right I have on my spirit, soul and body to the total and absolute control of the Holy Spirit. in Jesus name.
19. I hereby enroll myself from this moment in the full insurance coverage of the Holy Spirit to cover my life, my love and desires, to be fully paid with the blood of Jesus that was given to me at the time of my salvation in the name of Jesus.
20. Henceforth let no one trouble me, because I bear the blood of Jesus in my body.
21. I command the release of incredible wealth into my life in the name of Jesus.
22. Land yield your fullness to me in the name of Jesus.
23. Water yield your fullness to me in the name of Jesus.
24. Heaven open unto me, do not withhold my rain in due season in the name of Jesus.

25. Satan, I command you return every blessing you have stolen from me for the past three generations with commensurate interest in the name of Jesus.

26. World government, I decree henceforth, you shall not be able to make a law, regulation or decision that will limit my joy and happiness in the land of the living according to the will of God in the name of Jesus.

27. Fishes are created to live in the waters, gold in the ground and fowls in the air; I am created to live in the Garden of Eden, every voice suggesting otherwise I silence you permanently in the name of Jesus.

28. Aquariums are made for fishes, cages are made for birds, gold are made to shine, I decree in that name of Jesus that every power in heaven and earth shall work together for my comfort in the name of Jesus.

29. Dogs are not killed because they bark, birds are not destroyed because they fly, I shall not be destroyed or killed because of my destiny in the name of Jesus.

30. Gold is not destroyed because it shines, from now, I shall arise and shine for ever in the name of Jesus.

31. No mind shall be able to conceive my destruction in the name of Jesus.

32. As you did for Joseph & Moses let my enemies pay for the flight ticket to my place of prominence in the name of Jesus.

33. I shall not engage in a venture that will destroy my life, character and soul in the name of Jesus.

34. I command the heavens to release all my spiritual blessings whenever I need them in my journey of life in the name of Jesus.

35. God of Abraham, grant me the grace to enjoy the ministration of angels in a tangibly way in the name of Jesus.

36. Father do not hear the prayers nor honor the desires of my envious brethren when they ask for my downfall from you in the name of Jesus.

37. Father insulates me from discouragements from my fellow believers in the name of Jesus.

38. Father, deliver me from every form of religious demons in the name of Jesus.

39. Father let me never be in a position that will make me to deny you all the days of my life in the name of Jesus.

40. Fill my heart and my mouth with your praise all the days of my life in Jesus name.

41. Father, please grant me the grace to be faithful to you in my tithe and offerings in the name of Jesus.

42. Father, thank you for grace to pray and the promise of answers to my prayers in the name of Jesus. AMEN.

Chapter Nine

Deliverance from Third Party Covenant

a third party covenant is a covenant made on your behalf by someone who has authority over you. Covenants made by parents are always binding on their children until revoked, for instance the sin of Adam in Genesis Chapter three is the reason for the sins of all human race. *"All have sinned and come short of the glory of God"* Romans 3:23. Also leaders of nations, organizations or societies have authority to enter into covenants on behalf of their citizens. The choice of communism in China and the choice of Buddha, Hindu and Islam in Asia and the Middle East is a third party covenant that citizens under such leadership have to contend with. Extreme poverty and ignorance in Africa has made people to sacrifice the life of their loved ones to physical death or to slavery. Many towns and villages in Africa, Asia and other parts of the world are founded on bloodshed in the name of civil war, international wars or specific demand of Satan.

Cain killed his brother Abel. The Bible records in Hebrews that the blood of Abel was crying for vengeance against the wicked murder.

The sword did not depart from the house of David because of his unfaithful action against a faithful warrior, Uriah.

Isaiah 28:14-18 gives a very powerful insight into a truth that has kept people in perpetual bondage.

"Wherefore hear the word of the Lord, ye scornful men, that rule this people which is in Jerusalem.

Because ye have said, We have made a covenant with death, and with hell are we at agreement; when the overflowing scourge shall pass through, it shall not come unto us: for we have made lies our refuge, and under falsehood have we hid ourselves:

Therefore thus saith the Lord God, Behold, I lay in Zion for a foundation a stone, a tried stone, a precious corner stone, a sure foundation: he that believeth shall not make haste.

Judgment also will I lay to the line, and righteousness to the plummet: and the hail shall sweep away the refuge of lies, and the waters shall overflow the hiding place.

And your covenant with death shall be disannulled, and your agreement with hell shall not stand; when the overflowing scourge shall pass through, then ye shall be trodden down by it.

Some people have gone into a covenant with death and have made agreement with the grave against the life of other individuals. Human and animal sacrifices have been made to gain fame, money and power. This is very common in Africa and Asia. Scornful men that ruled the

people of God according to verse 14 have entered into covenants with death and agreements with the grave so they could perpetrate evil and not be judged. Some people have sacrificed their children or other innocent blood because they desire power or position. In Exodus, King Herod at the time of Moses, slew innocent children in order to perpetuate his hold on power. Another Herod repeated the same thing at the time of Jesus Christ, in order to kill baby Jesus. **Jer. 17:9 says:**
"The heart is deceitful above all things and desperately wicked: who can know it?" So many African leaders living and dead have shown this desperate wickedness. The West is also not spared in this wickedness. For instance, the late President J F Kennedy's life was wasted for the reason only known to the killer.

Ignorance is never an excuse for failure, the Bible says, you shall know the truth, and the truth that you know will set you free. The word of God admonishes us not to be unaware of the devices of Satan. Esau placed a death sentence on Jacob, only intense prayers set him free. Man is created to live in the Garden of Eden, and not in the garden of torments and confusion. Some people have entered into a covenant to do business that will destroy the lives of innocent children, cities and nations. Satan has employees who are well paid to steal, kill and destroy the lives of innocent babies. It took God the pain of sacrificing His only son to grant you and I the freedom from every form of oppression. All you need now is your mouth and your heart. According to Jeremiah 29:12-14:

Then shall ye call upon me, and ye shall go and pray unto me, and I will hearken unto you. And ye shall seek me, and find me, when ye shall search for me with all your heart.
And I will be found of you, saith the Lord: and I will turn away your captivity, and I will gather you from all the nations, and from all the places whither I have driven you, saith the Lord; and I will bring you again into the place whence I caused you to be carried away captive.

God is faithful, He hears and answers prayers.

Please pray these prayers very aggressively until you receive a tangible confirmation of an answer.

1. Father I receive the gift of a foundation, a stone, a tried stone, a precious corner stone, a sure foundation that you laid in Zion for me in the name of Jesus.
2. Father I believe and receive the provision of your son Jesus Christ of Nazareth for my deliverance from every curse in the name of Jesus.
3. In Jesus name I have redemption through His blood, the forgiveness of sins, according to the riches of His grace.
4. I am blessed with all spiritual blessings in the heavenly places in Christ Jesus.

5. From henceforth let no man trouble me: for I bear in my body the marks of the Lord Jesus.

6. I am free from every shame and guilt as a result of all wickedness against my life in the name of Jesus.

7. Ye scornful men that have been ruling my life, hear the word of the Lord, you shall be judged according to your evil intention towards me in the name of Jesus.

8. Hail, sweep away every refuge of lies against my life in the name of Jesus.

9. Waters, overflow the hiding place of all evil, sicknesses and diseases in my body and my entire life in the name of Jesus.

10. I decree in the name of Jesus, every arrow of destruction targeted and fired at me shall be returned to the sender of such arrows in the name of Jesus.

11. Every covenant entered with death against my love, peace and joy shall be disannulled in the name of Jesus.

12. I cancel every agreement with hell against my life in the name of Jesus.

13. I decree in the name of Jesus, that every eater of my flesh shall begin to eat their own flesh in the name of Jesus.

14. Every sucker of my blood shall begin to drink their own blood in the name of Jesus.

15. I decree in the name of Jesus that all prison doors shut against me shall begin to open unto me on their own accord in the name of Jesus.

16. No weapon fashioned against me shall prosper and every evil tongue against my progress is hereby condemned in the name of Jesus.

17. Surely there is no enchantment against me, neither is their any divination against my future in the name of Jesus.

18. I am anointed of the Lord, so kings and lords shall be reproved for my sake, no man shall be able to execute any evil agenda upon my life in Jesus name.

19. My life shall move in the direction of fruitfulness and dominion in the name of Jesus.

20. I shall not be moved away from the parameters of the safety of God in the name of Jesus.

21. I clear my pipe created to receive the rivers of living water of any form of debris like hate, jealousy, laziness, lies, immoral sexual activities and idolatry in the name of Jesus.

22. I shall not disappoint my holy angels in the name of Jesus.

23. I shall not be separated from the presence of God in the name of Jesus.

24. Holy Ghost, restrict me from all activities that will grief you in the name of Jesus.

25. I receive joy devoid of any form of sorrow in the name of Jesus.

26. My destiny is sealed with the Holy Spirit of promise in the name of Jesus.

27. It is written in Psalm 18:45 " The strangers shall fade away, and be afraid out of their close places " I

command every strange spirit interfering with my life to depart now and never to return in the name of Jesus.

28. Every unclean spirit supporting any act of disobedience to God and His Word in my life, I cast you away in the name of Jesus.

29. According to Micah 4:4 *But they shall sit every man under his vine and under his fig tree; and none shall make them afraid*", no power shall force me out of my place of comfort, joy, happiness, freedom and peace in Jesus name.

30. Oh God of restoration restore to me the years that the locust had eaten, the cankerworm, and the caterpillar, and the palmerworm in the name of Jesus.

31. The hands of mine (mention your name) have laid the foundation of this house (my success, marriage, career etc) my hands shall also finish it, and the whole world will know that the Lord of hosts has sent me in the name of Jesus.

32. I expunge by power of the Holy Spirit every failure programmed into my future by any authorities in the name of Jesus.

33. The seed of greatness in Abraham was not destroyed in Egypt; every seed of greatness in me shall not be destroyed in any situation or condition I found myself in the name of Jesus.

34. Money, Fame and Power hear the word of the Lord, you shall not tempt me to sin against God in the name of Jesus.

35. Father save me from every torment as a result of my personal disobedience to your word.

36. Every organ of my body, I command you, do not obey cancer, kidney disease or heart problem, you must obey the word of God that says, "by His stripes you are healed" in the name of Jesus.

37. I shall live in health and prosperity as my soul prospers in the name of Jesus.

38. I turn myself to the light of God; my presence shall cast away every forms of darkness and scatter the congregation of unclean spirits in the name of Jesus.

39. I am a terror to the kingdom of darkness in the name of Jesus.

40. Oh Lord my God, make a name for yourself with my whole life in the name of Jesus Christ.

Chapter Ten

Songs of Deliverance

Good day to you my dear Jesus 2x
You are the way, the truth and the life
Good day to you my dear Jesus.

Jesus, Jesus, Jesus. 2x
Kings of kings and lord of lords
Jesus, Jesus, Jesus.

Come into my heart oh lord, I pray 2x
Come into my heart and dwell with me
Come into my heart oh lord, I pray

Come into my life and open my eyes 2x
Open my eyes to know you more
Come into my life and open my eyes.

Come into my life and save my soul 2x
Let my soul be your fertile ground
Come into my life and save my soul

Come into my life and heal my pains 2x
Come into my life and make me whole
Come into my life and heal my pains

Make wars to cease in all my life 2x
Let there be peace all around me
Make wars to cease in all my life.

Destroy the works of evil in my life 2x
For this reason you were manifested
Destroy the works of evil in my life.

Root up foreign plants in my life 2x
For they are not planted by you
Root up foreign plants in my life

Come into my life and take control 2x
Take control of my entire life
Come into my life and take control

Come into my life and change my life 2x
Let it line up with your will
Come into my life and change my life

Do a new thing in my life 2x
Let my enemies be confounded
Do a new thing in my life

Blow them off and destroy them 2x
Forces contending with my life
Blow them off and destroy them

Arise today scatter your enemies 2x
All your enemies in my life
Arise today scatter your enemies

Come into my life to prosper me 2x
Let me flourish like your vine
Come into my life to prosper me

Come into me and make me your friend 2x
Delight yourself in my praises
Come into me and make me your friend

Guide me lead me and teach me your ways 2x
Watch over me with you own eyes
Guide me lead me and teach me your ways.

Amen amen so shall it be 2x
Your words are ye and amen
Amen amen so shall it be.

This hymn was written in the year, 2002 at my duty post as a Security Officer at the American Hearts Association in Dallas Texas. Please sing it and use each stanza as a prayer point.

Pastor Adebayo is a graduate of The Redeemed Christian Church of God Bible College, and an Ordained Pastor. He holds a Bachelor's degree in Chemical Engineering from Obafemi Awolowo University in Nigeria. He is a Licensed Individual Asbestos Consultant in the State of Texas, USA.

He was the first Head of Men's Ministry of RCCG, Household of Faith in Arlington Texas, USA. He was also the head of prayer warriors at RCCG Household of Faith, and RCCG Eagle Believers Chapel in the Dallas area of Texas in the United States of America, before he was called to start RCCG, The Winners Assembly where he is a parish Pastor. He is currently the Prayer Secretary of Texas One, The Headquarter Zone, of the Redeemed Christian of God North America.

He is married to Deaconess Elizabeth Adebayo and they are blessed with children. He is an international itinerary minister and a prayer warrior.